Stories from the Quran
Book 3

Joseph *(Yusuf)* in the Well
&
Moses *(Musa)* in the Cradle

written by
Noura Durkee

illustrated by
Fatima Masood

HOOD HOOD BOOKS

Joseph in the Well

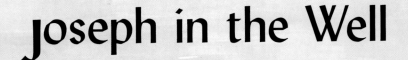

Joseph was a very special boy.
Joseph's father, Jacob, knew that his son
would one day become
a wise Prophet.

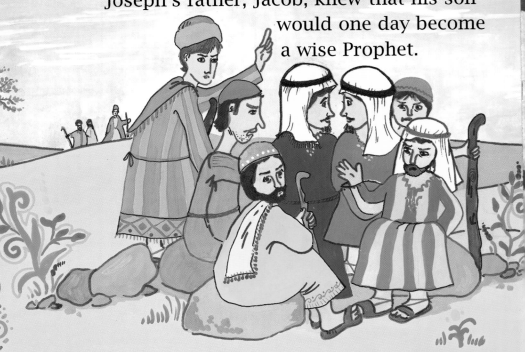

Joseph's big brothers were jealous of him.
They huddled together in a corner.
They said to each other,
"Let's get him! Let's throw him away!"

They went to Jacob and said,
"Father, let Joseph come to play
with us in the hills."

Jacob did not want to let
Joseph out of his sight.
He was afraid something
would happen to him.

At last, he let him go.

The brothers walked
far away up to the hills.
It was beautiful up there.
The sun was shining and
the birds were singing.

Suddenly, the naughty brothers
grabbed Joseph.
They threw him down a well,
and ran all the way
back home!

They told their father
an animal ate him.
But their father did not
believe them at all.
He prayed that Joseph was safe.

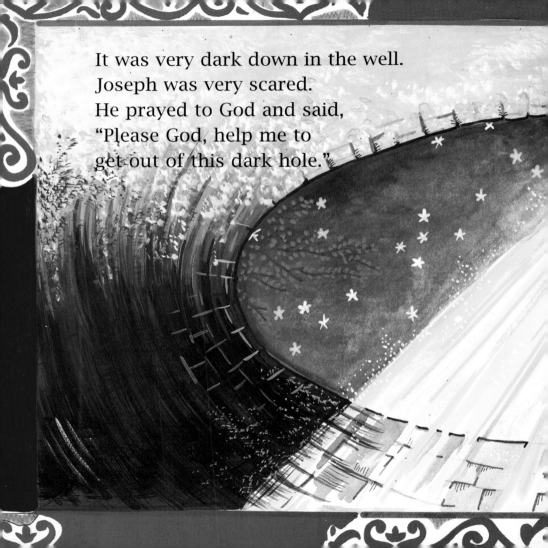

It was very dark down in the well.
Joseph was very scared.
He prayed to God and said,
"Please God, help me to
get out of this dark hole."

Joseph waited
for a long, long time.

At last, a camel caravan came by.
They looked for water in the well,
and found Joseph!
Joseph was very happy.
God had answered
his prayers.

The people took him with them
far away, to a land called Egypt.

Joseph grew up in Egypt,
and after many adventures,
he became a Prince and a Prophet.
Much later, he met his whole family again.
He hugged his father and mother,
and forgave his brothers.

Moses
in the Cradle

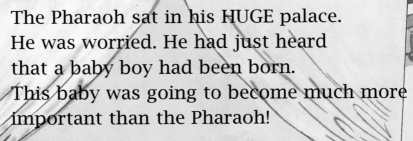

The Pharaoh sat in his HUGE palace.
He was worried. He had just heard
that a baby boy had been born.
This baby was going to become much more
important than the Pharaoh!

The Pharaoh ordered his soldiers
to capture and kill him!

Moses' mother heard the news.
She was worried for her baby.
She had to hide him from the soldiers.
God told her to weave a basket for
him. Quickly she twisted
the reeds and grasses.

She made the basket
strong on the outside,
and soft on the inside.

She covered it with
sticky stuff so the water
would not get in.
It was like a little
boat.

Mother fed Baby Moses well.
She did not want him to cry.
She put him in the cradle.
She kissed him goodbye.

God had promised her that
he would keep Moses safe.
Carefully, she put the cradle
into the river. Moses
smiled and closed his eyes.

The cradle bobbed up and
down in the water.
Moses slept peacefully.
He did not see the big birds,
or the frogs, or the fishes.

He did not see the palm trees
waving overhead.

He did not even see the Egyptian ladies
coming down to bathe.

The ladies took off their slippers
and put their feet in the river.
Then they saw the cradle!
They waded into the water,
and pulled it to the bank.

"Oh! A baby!" they cried.
"Let's show him to the Queen."
The Queen loved Moses.
She took him to the palace and
raised him as a Prince.

Many adventures later,
Moses became a great Prophet.

Copyright © Hood Hood Books 2000

Hood Hood Books
46 Clabon Mews
London SW1X 0EH

Tel 44 (0) 20 7584 7878
Fax: 44 (0) 20 7225 0386
E-mail: info@hoodhood.com
Web Site: www.hoodhood.com

British Library Cataloguing-in-Publication Data
A catalogue record for this book is available from the British Library

ISBN 1 900251 55 8

Origination by *Fine Line Graphics Ltd.* - London
Printed by *Khai Wah-Ferco Pte. Ltd.* - Singapore

PUBLISHER'S NOTE

According to the *hadith* (saying) of the Prophet Muhammad, peace be upon him, it is traditional practice not to depict God's Angels, Messengers and Prophets in any form of visual representation. There are no such depictions in this book.